P9-BZQ-249

In memory of my grandfather, Isaac Godlin
—H.Z.

For my three amusing boys
—K.G.

Text copyright © 2008 by Harriet Ziefert

Illustrations copyright © 2008 by Karla Gudeon

All rights reserved / CIP Data is available.

Published in the United States 2008 by

Blue Apple Books, 515 Valley Street, Maplewood, N.J. 07040

www.blueapplebooks.com

Distributed in the U.S. by Chronicle Books

First Edition

Printed in China

ISBN: 978-1-934706-33-6

2 4 6 8 10 9 7 5 3 1

# Hanukkah Haiku

Harriet Ziefert

paintings by
Karla Gudeon

Haddonfield Public Library
60 Haddon Ave.
Haddonfield, N.J. 08033

Blue Apple Books

**1**

For eight days and nights,
special candles we will light.
It is Hanukkah.

**2**

Two candles tonight.
Daddy holds the Shammash high.
It lights the others.

**3**

Three candles tonight.
Mommy makes a dreidel spin.
Nun, gimel, hey, shin.

Four candles tonight.
Grandma fries the latkes brown.
We want applesauce.

5

Five candles tonight.
Uncle gives a gift of gelt.
The coins are shiny.

**6**

Six candles tonight.
We listen to the story
of the Maccabees.

**7**

Seven lights tonight.
We hold hands and dance and turn.
It is Hanukkah.

Eight candles tonight.
Happy children stand and gaze.
All the candles blaze.

# Blessing the Hanukkah Candles

The candles are arranged in the Menorah from right to left,
but they are always lit from left to right.
The Shammash candle is lit first.
It is used to light the others.
While the Shammash is being held,
the blessings are said in Hebrew, English, or both.

"Barukh Ata Adonai, Eloheynu Melekh ha'olam,
asher kidushanu b'mizvotav, v'tzivanu l'hadlik
ner shel Hanukkah.

Praised are You, Lord, Our God, Ruler of Creation,
Who has made us holy through His commandments,
and commanded us to kindle the Hanukkah lights.

Barukh Ata Adonai, Eloheynu Melekh ha'olam, she'asa nisim
l'avoteynu, ba'yamim ha'haym ba'zman hazeh.

Praised are You, Lord, Our God, Ruler of Creation,
Who worked miracles for our ancestors during times past
at this season."

After all the candles are lit, from left to right, "Hanerot Hallu" is recited:

"We light these candles in memory of the miracles, the remarkable events, the redemptions, and the victories which You granted our forefathers in days past through Your holy priests. Throughout the eight days of Hanukkah, these lights are holy. We may not use them for everyday tasks. We may only look at them, so that we may be reminded to offer thanks and praise to Your glorious Name for Your miracles, Your wonders, and Your deliverance."

Then the hymn "Maoz Tzur" or "Rock of Ages," written in the thirteenth century by a poet named Mordechai, concludes the ceremony:

"Rock of ages, let our song praise Thy saving power;
Thou amidst the raging foes were our sheltering tower.
Furious they assailed us when Thine arm availed us,
And Thy word broke their sword,
When our own strength failed us.
*Maoz Tzur!*"

HADDONFIELD PUBLIC LIBRARY

3 7286 00086044 7

YP 296.435 ZIE
Ziefert, Harriet.

Hanukkah haiku